NORTH DAKOTA

in words and pictures

BY DENNIS B. FRADIN

MAPS BY LEN W. MEENTS

Consultant:
Frank E. Vyzralek
State Archivist
State Historical Society of
North Dakota, Bismarck

 CHILDRENS PRESS, CHICAGO

*For my friend and
editor, Joan Downing*

For their help, the author thanks:
Gerianne Davis, Assistant Director of the North Dakota Indian Affairs Commission
Marilyn Hudson, Bureau of Indian Affairs, Fort Berthold Agency
Dr. Larry Loendorf, Department of Anthropology and Archaeology, University of North Dakota
Chandler Forman
Frank E. Vyzralek, State Archivist, State Historical Society of North Dakota
Connie Sylvester, Historical Assistant, State Historical Society of North Dakota
Jim Fuglie, Assistant to North Dakota Agriculture Commissioner

The Red River of the North

Library of Congress Cataloging in Publication Data

Fradin, Dennis B
  North Dakota in words and pictures.

  SUMMARY: Introduces the history, geography, indus-
tries, cities, and major tourist attractions of the
Flickertail State.
1. North Dakota—Juvenile literature. |1. North
Dakota| I. Meents, Len W.   II. Title
F636.3F7   978.4   80-26480
ISBN 0-516-03934-2

Picture Acknowledgments:
UNITED STATES DEPARTMENT OF AGRICULTURE PHOTO: Cover
GRAND FORKS CHAMBER OF COMMERCE: pages 2, 13, 18 (left), 25, 40
JAMES P. ROWAN: pages 5, 6 (right), 9 (right), 10, 36 (left)
PHOTOS COURTESY OF NORTH DAKOTA TOURISM PROMOTION
DIVISION: pages 6 (left), 9 (left), 14, 18 (right), 19, 22, 26, 28, 29, 30, 32,
34, 36 (right), 38
JAMESTOWN CHAMBER OF COMMERCE: pages 11 (right), 16, 17
BISMARCK AREA CHAMBER OF COMMERCE: page 11 (left)
MINOT CONVENTION AND VISITORS BUREAU: pages 37, 42
AMERICAN NATURAL RESOURCES COMPANY, DETROIT, MI: pages
20, 21
COVER: Wheat harvesting in North Dakota

North Dakota

The Sioux (SOO) Indians called themselves the *Dakota* (dah • KOH • tah). Dakota means "friends." North Dakota was named for that Indian word.

North Dakota has flat lands. They stretch as far as the eye can see. North Dakota is a farming and ranching state. It is a leading state for growing wheat, barley, and rye. Beef cattle are raised on North Dakota ranches.

Do you know where the exact center of North America is located? Or where there is a "peace garden" that is partly in Canada? Do you know where home-run hitter Roger Maris (MARE • iss) grew up? Or where Garrison Dam is located?

If you haven't guessed, the answer to all these questions is: North Dakota!

Millions of years ago, dinosaurs (DINE • ah • sores) roamed through what is now North Dakota. Triceratops (tri • SARE • ah • tops) was there. Three horns on his head kept him safe from other dinosaurs. The last dinosaurs died long ago. But their bones have been found. In 1963 a triceratops skeleton was found in North Dakota.

About one million years ago the weather turned cold. The Ice Age began. Mountains of ice, called *glaciers* (GLAY • sherz), moved down from the north. They covered most of North Dakota. The glaciers ground up rocks into rich soil. They spread the soil across the land. Thanks largely to glaciers, North Dakota has great farmland today.

The first people came to North Dakota at least 12,000 years ago. They lived by hunting large animals. Their stone tools have been found in North Dakota.

In more recent times, many Indian tribes lived in North Dakota. Some were the Arikara (ah • RICK • ah • rah), the Hidatsa (hih • DOT • sah), and the Mandan (MAN • dan). They were tribes that farmed. They grew corn, beans, and squash. Farming Indians settled in the valley of the Missouri River. They built villages. They lived in earth lodges. The lodges were made of logs covered by brush and dirt.

Restored Mandan earth lodges at the Slant Indian Village near Mandan

There are still a few buffalo in North Dakota, and tepees can be found in the Plains Indian Village at the Fort Union National Historic Site.

The Sioux were a hunting people. They hunted on horseback. They rode after buffalo. They killed the buffalo with bows and arrows. The Sioux used all parts of the buffalo. The meat was eaten. The bones were made into tools. The skins were used to make clothes and *tepees.* A tepee was a tent made of about 15 buffalo hides.

In 1682 a Frenchman named La Salle claimed much of America for France. This included part of North Dakota. La Salle never entered North Dakota.

Pierre de la Verendrye (PYAIR dee lah vay • rahn • DREE) was the first known explorer there. He was a French-Canadian. He came down from Canada in 1738. His three sons came with him. Vérendrye met friendly Mandan Indians. Four years later two of his sons came back. They explored some more.

Beavers and other furry animals lived in North Dakota. Their furs were worth a lot of money. They were used to make clothes. In the late 1700s and early 1800s fur traders came to North Dakota. They traded whiskey and trinkets to the Indians. In return they received the animal furs. In 1797 Charles Chaboillez (shah • bwah • LAY) set up a fur-trading post at Pembina (PEHM • bih • nah). Soon more trading posts were built. French, Canadian, English, and American fur traders all came to North Dakota.

In 1803 the United States bought a lot of land from France. Part of North Dakota was included. President Thomas Jefferson wanted to learn about the lands now owned by the United States. He sent two men to explore. Their names were Meriwether Lewis (MARE • ih • weth • uhr LOO • iss) and William Clark. Lewis and Clark left from near St. Louis, Missouri (SAINT LOO • iss, mih • ZOO • ree). They headed west. They went toward the Pacific Ocean. On the way, they passed through North Dakota.

Lewis and Clark built Fort Mandan in North Dakota. Nearby they met a young Indian woman. Her name was Sacajawea (sock • ah • jah • WAY • ah). In North Dakota she is known as Sakakawea (suh • KAH • kah • wee • ah). She went with them on their journey. Sacajawea helped them speak to Indians they met. She helped get food and horses from Indian people. Sacajawea led them all the way to the Pacific Ocean.

Lewis and Clark built Fort Mandan (above). A statue of their Indian guide, Sakakawea, stands on the capitol grounds in Bismarck (left).

Lewis and Clark reported that the North Dakota region had good soil. But many Americans back east thought that North Dakota was useless land. Some called it part of the "Great American Desert."

In 1818 the United States made a treaty with England. The treaty gave the United States the rest of North Dakota. The United States now owned all of North Dakota. It wasn't a state yet. It was land owned by the United States.

The old blockhouse at Fort Abraham Lincoln State Park has been restored. Fort Abraham Lincoln is only one of the many forts built in the 1800s to protect travelers and settlers.

For many years, fur traders were just about the only non-Indians in North Dakota. But people did pass through North Dakota. They were on their way to other places. Forts were built to protect the travelers.

In 1861 the United States formed the Dakota Territory (TARE • ih • tore • ee). It included what are now the states of North and South Dakota. Parts of Montana (mahn • TAN • ah) and Wyoming (wye • OH • ming) were also in the Dakota Territory.

The United States government wanted Americans to settle in the Dakota Territory. In 1862 the government passed the Homestead (HOME • sted) Act. Free land was offered to settlers. Some people moved to North Dakota. They planted seeds and hoped for the best. The crops grew better than people had hoped!

More people set out for North Dakota in the 1870s. The people traveled in wagons pulled by oxen. They piled furniture, clothes, and everything that would fit into the wagons. When they got to North Dakota, the

Modern-day pioneers made a wagon-train stop near Jamestown during the country's Bicentennial year (below). A statue of a pioneer family on the capitol grounds (left) honors the original pioneers.

people built houses. Where there were trees, they built them of wood. But in most places there were no trees for miles. That didn't stop the settlers. They cut up the hard ground, called *sod,* into brick-sized pieces. They piled up the sod bricks to form walls. After a lot of hard work, the sod house was finished. The house kept the family warm in the winter and cool in the summer.

Most of the settlers farmed. They planted wheat. Wheat grew very well in North Dakota. Some wheat farms in the Red River Valley were very large. They were called *bonanza* farms.

Some people who came to North Dakota became teachers. Some became storekeepers. Churches and schools were built. Towns grew. Fargo (FAR • go), Bismarck (BIHZ • mark), Grand Forks, and Jamestown (JAYMZ • town) were four towns built in the 1870s. They were all built when railroads were entering North Dakota.

Early scenes of Grand Forks, one of the North Dakota towns built in the 1870s

A pioneer town has been recreated at Bonanzaville USA in West Fargo. Actual buildings from early Red River towns have been brought here and restored. These pictures show an old hotel (right), an old locomotive (below left), and an old schoolhouse (below right).

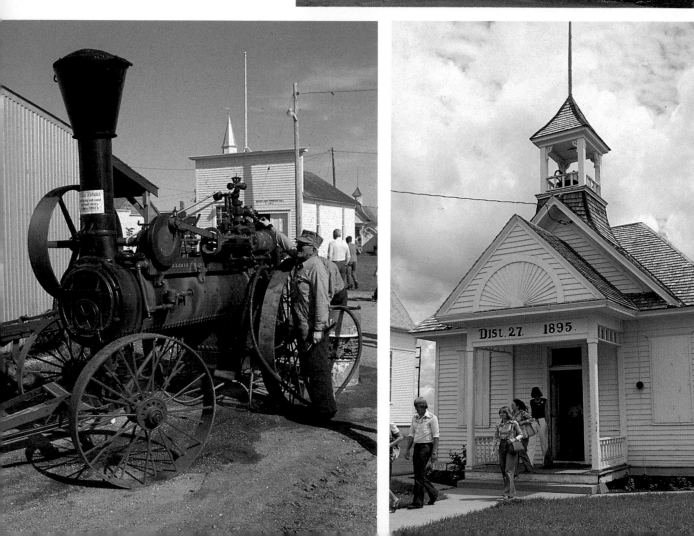

The Indians grew angry as settlers took their lands. In nearby Minnesota (mihn • eh • SOTE • ah) and Montana there were huge battles. Some Indians in North Dakota fought to keep their lands. There were many soldiers against them. The Indians were forced onto reservations (rehz • uhr • VAY • shunz).

Indian fighting finally ended. Then even more people came to North Dakota. In the 1870s and 1880s railroads were built. Trains carried farm products out of North Dakota. They brought people into the region. The population grew. Many people wanted North Dakota to become a state.

North Dakota was made a state on November 2, 1889. That same day South Dakota also became a state. President Benjamin Harrison (BEHN • jah • mihn HARE • ih • suhn) covered the names of the states when he signed the papers. Not even he knew which one he signed first! Both states claim to be the thirty-ninth state.

Cattle grazing on typical North Dakota prairie land.

Bismarck had been the capital of the Dakota
Territory. Now it was made capital of North Dakota.
North Dakota was nicknamed the *Flickertail State*. That
is because ground squirrels, called "flickertails," live in
the state.

Some people in the new state set up cattle ranches.
Cowboys on horseback watched the cattle. They rounded
up the cattle. Then they branded them. That way people
could see which ranch owned the cattle. Cowboys carried
guns. They were mostly used to keep coyotes and wolves

away from the cattle. The cattle were worth a lot of money. They were sent to other states to be made into meat.

Farmers began to grow other crops besides wheat. You remember those people who had called North Dakota a useless "desert." Their grandchildren were now eating many foods from North Dakota.

North Dakota farmers had hard times in the late 1800s and early 1900s. Floods ruined farms in some years. In 1897 floods swept away farm buildings and

Farmland near Jamestown

The farm machines of today are even more efficient than the ones developed during the early 1900s.

livestock in the Red River Valley. In the 1930s, there were droughts (DROWTZ). These were times of little or no rain. Without rain, crops died. In some years, millions of grasshoppers filled the air. The grasshoppers landed in farmers' fields. They ate the crops. In 1931, hungry grasshoppers even ate wooden farm tools!

During the 1900s North Dakotans had to find ways to solve farm problems. New seeds were developed. They grew into bigger and better crops. Machines were built. They helped farmers plant and harvest crops faster. Many areas did not have enough rain. There, *dry farming* was done. Farmers plowed their soil so that it would hold what little water was there.

Dams were also built. During dry times, dams release water to farms. Dams also turn waterpower into electricity. The Garrison Dam was completed in 1954. It is on the Missouri River. It is one of the biggest dams in the world. The Garrison Diversion Project (GARE • ih • suhn dih • VUHR • zhun PRAH • jeckt) was begun in 1967. It brings water to farms in a large area of North Dakota.

Today, North Dakota is an important farming state. It is the second leading wheat-growing state. It is also the

The Garrison Dam (left) is one of the biggest dams in the world. Irrigation systems (below) are important to North Dakota farmers.

second leading rye-growing state. It is the number one state for growing barley.

In 1951 another treasure besides food came from North Dakota ground. This was oil. Oil is used to run cars and machinery. By the 1970s, oil was coming from a number of wells in North Dakota. Natural gas and coal are also mined in the state.

You have learned about some of North Dakota's history. Now it is time for a trip—in words and pictures—through the Flickertail State.

North Dakota is shaped much like a rectangle. Another country—Canada—is to the north of North

Lignite (brown coal) is mined in North Dakota (below).

Flat land, or plains, of North Dakota

Dakota. Minnesota is to the east, across the Red River. South Dakota is its neighbor (NAY • buhr) to the south. Montana is to the west.

Pretend you're in an airplane high above North Dakota. Do you see how flat the land looks? Such flat land is called a *plain.* Most of the state is made up of plains. But you will see some hills in North Dakota.

Your airplane is landing in a city in the eastern part of the state. This is Fargo. It lies on the Red River. That is a big farming area. Fargo is North Dakota's biggest city. North Dakota doesn't have any really big cities. The 59,000 people of Fargo could fit into a big football stadium!

Fargo was founded in 1871. The city was named for William G. Fargo. He was a partner in Wells, Fargo & Company. That was a famous company that sent people, gold, and silver by stagecoach.

Tractors and other farm machines are made in Fargo. Crops grown in the Red River Valley are sent to Fargo. There they are packaged as food. Cattle are sent to nearby West Fargo. There they are made into many meat products.

Visit Bonanzaville (buh • NAN • zuh • vill). It is in West

This log cabin is one of many pioneer buildings in Bonanzaville USA.

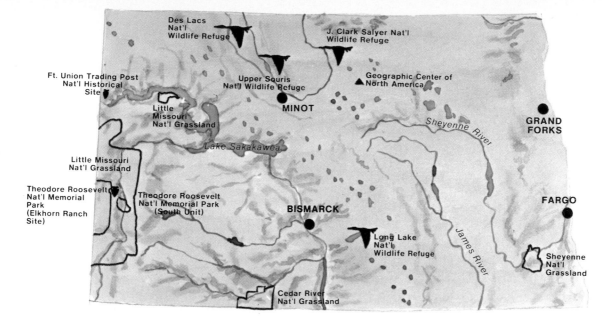

Fargo. It is made up of over 30 buildings. Bonanzaville looks like a pioneer North Dakota town of the 1880s. It has houses, stores, and other buildings. The buildings were taken from old towns in the area. You will also enjoy Trollwood (TROLE • wood) Park in Fargo. Plays and musical events are held there during the summer.

You will see many students in Fargo. North Dakota State University is in the city.

Fargo is in the Red River Valley. This big valley has some of the world's best farmland. Many thousands of years ago a lake covered the Red River Valley. This lake, called Lake Agassiz (AG • ah • zee), drained away. But it left some great soil in the Red River Valley.

The Red River Valley is nicknamed the "Bread Basket of the World." A lot of wheat is grown there. Much of the wheat is made into bread. A lot of barley and rye are also grown in the valley.

These crops are grown elsewhere in the state, too. Head west from Fargo. You will see farms in many areas of North Dakota. Most North Dakotans live on farms or in farm areas. There are about 40,000 farms and ranches in the state.

It would be fun to visit some North Dakota farms. Farming is a science today. Some farmers use computers (kum • PYOO • terz). Computers tell farmers how much seed to use. They also tell them the best way to grow the crops. Farmers use many machines. Tractors are used to pull heavy equipment. Machines called *drills* are used to plant seeds. Machines called *combines* (KAHM • bynz) are used to harvest crops.

You will see big buildings called *grain elevators* (EHL • eh • vay • terz) in North Dakota towns. The farmers bring their wheat and other grains to the grain elevators. The grain is stored there. Later, the grain is sent to food factories.

You might want to know what kinds of foods are made from North Dakota crops. You remember that some North Dakota wheat is used to make bread. Wheat is also used to make noodles and breakfast cereals. Oats from North Dakota are used to make breakfast cereals, too. Barley is used to make beer and livestock feed. Livestock feed, cereal, and rye bread are three products made from the rye. Did you ever eat sunflower seeds? Did you ever use cooking oil made from sunflower seeds? North Dakota is a leading state for raising sunflowers as a crop.

A field of sunflowers near Grand Forks

Among the many events
that take place during
North Dakota rodeos
are bronc riding (right),
barrel riding (below right),
and bull riding (below).

You would enjoy a visit to a North Dakota cattle ranch. Cowboys tend the cattle. Some still work on horseback. Others use trucks or airplanes to watch the herds.

Ranching is a science, too. Cowboys and ranchers raise cattle that will produce high-grade beef. They work to keep the cattle healthy.

The cowboys know how to have fun, too. They still hold rodeos. At these events, they see who can rope cattle the fastest. They see who can stay on broncos and bulls the longest. The Roughrider Festival (RUFF • rye • der FESS • tih • vuhl) at Dickinson (DIK • ihn • suhn) is just one of the state's many rodeos.

Even in the cities you can tell that North Dakota is mainly a farming and ranching state. Factories in North Dakota cities turn farm and ranch products into food.

Visit the city of Jamestown. It is about 100 miles west of Fargo. Jamestown lies in the valley of the James River. It was first settled in the 1870s.

The "World's Largest Buffalo" in Jamestown

Farm machines are made in Jamestown. Frozen bread dough is made there. Other food products are also made in the city.

In Jamestown you can see the "World's Largest Buffalo." It isn't a real buffalo. It's a statue that is 26 feet high and weighs 120,000 pounds. It is a reminder that millions of buffalo once roamed through North Dakota.

As you go through North Dakota, you will see many real animals. There are still some buffalo. Deer can be seen in many places. Prairie (PRARE • ee) dogs can also be seen. They aren't really dogs. They are in the squirrel

This prairie dog has come out of his tunnel to look around.

family. Prairie dogs live together in "dog towns." They dig tunnels in the ground. If a hungry coyote (kye • OH • tee) comes along, they head home to their tunnels!

You might hear coyotes howling on the North Dakota plains. Foxes, beavers, and raccoons are some of the other animals that live in the state. Pronghorn antelopes also live in North Dakota. They can run very fast—up to 60 miles per hour.

Go about 100 miles west of Jamestown. You will come to the city of Bismarck. Bismarck is the capital of North Dakota. The city lies along the Missouri River.

Once, Mandan Indians lived here. The town of Bismarck began in 1872. Bismarck was made capital of the Dakota Territory in 1883. It has been capital of the state of North Dakota since 1889.

You can see the state capitol building in Bismarck for many miles. The building is 18 stories tall. It is nicknamed the "Skyscraper of the Prairies."

Outside the capitol building there is a statue of Sakakawea. She was the Indian woman who guided Lewis and Clark. A statue of a pioneer family is a reminder of the early settlers. There is also a statue of John Burke. He was a North Dakota governor.

You will enjoy the inside of the capitol building, too. North Dakota lawmakers meet there. In recent years they have worked on laws to make better schools and highways for North Dakota. They have worked on laws to provide water for farmland. They have also worked to keep North Dakota's air and water clean.

Many Bismarck people work in government. Others work at making meat products and farm equipment.

There is much to do in Bismarck. The Dakota Zoo is fun. There is a prairie dog town in the zoo. You can also see buffalo there. The North Dakota Heritage Center is in Bismarck. There you can learn about North Dakota Indians and pioneers.

The city of Mandan is just west of Bismarck. Near Mandan, visit the Fort Abraham Lincoln State Park. General George A. Custer was stationed at Fort Abraham Lincoln in the 1870s. From there, he led soldiers in fights against the Indians. In 1876 Custer and his men left to fight the Sioux. Custer and over 250 of his men were killed. That was in the famous Battle of the Little Bighorn in nearby Montana.

People like to swim, sail, and fish
in North Dakota's lakes and rivers.
Above: Sailing on Lake Sakakawea.
Right: Fishing along the Missouri River.

Northwest of Fort Abraham Lincoln you will see Lake
Sakakawea. It is the biggest lake in North Dakota. The
lake is formed by waters held back by the Garrison Dam.

North Dakota has many smaller lakes. Some were
formed long ago by melting glaciers. People like to swim
and boat in North Dakota's lakes. Many like to fish.
Even in the bitter-cold winters, some people fish. They
cut a hole in the ice. Then they fish through the hole.

In the spring and summer, many birds enjoy North Dakota's lakes. You may see ducks and geese splashing around. Each year, millions of waterfowl are born in North Dakota.

Visit the Fort Berthold (BIRTH • hold) Indian Reservation, on Lake Sakakawea. Mandan, Hidatsa, and Arikara Indians live there.

A reservation is land reserved for the Indians. There are four Indian reservations in North Dakota. About 18,000 Indians live on the reservations. About 7,000 live elsewhere in the state.

Five main tribes live in North Dakota today. Besides the Mandan, Hidatsa, and Arikara, there are the Sioux and the Chippewa (CHIP • uh • wah).

Indian people have many different jobs. Many are ranchers. A number own small farms. There are Indian doctors, lawyers, and teachers. You can also find Indians in many different businesses.

These Indian children danced at a powwow.

The Indian people maintain old customs. Children are taught English as well as their Indian language. Grandparents tell children stories of their people. In the summer, powwows are held. At these get-togethers there are dances, games, and sports. There are also "naming ceremonies" at powwows. This is when Indian children are given the names they will have for life. Each of the five main tribes has its own special ceremony.

After seeing the Indian reservation, head west into the Badlands. The Badlands are made up of soft rock carved by water and wind over many years. You will see many strange rock formations in the Badlands. You will see *buttes* (BYOOTZ). These are hills that stand alone. They are not part of a mountain range. White Butte, in the Badlands, is 3,506 feet above sea level. It is the highest point in the state.

At night, you can see strange glowing lights in the Badlands. They come from the Burning Lignite (LIHG • nyte) Beds. Lignite is a kind of coal. The Burning Lignite Beds have been on fire for many years. Some of the fires were started by lightning. Others may have been started by Indian and pioneer campfires.

In the 1880s, a man named Theodore Roosevelt (THEE • uh • dore ROSE • uh • vehlt) had two ranches in the Badlands. He tended cattle. He hunted buffalo. He liked to ride his horse through the Badlands. Once, Roosevelt helped track down a group of outlaws. In 1901 Roosevelt became the twenty-sixth president of the United States.

Theodore Roosevelt National
Memorial Park in the Badlands
is a good place to go trail riding.

Theodore Roosevelt National Memorial Park is in the
Badlands. It is named after the president. You can ride a
horse there, just as Theodore Roosevelt did. You will see
many wild animals in the park. There are buffalo, deer,
foxes, coyotes, and prairie dogs.

From the Badlands, head northeast. You will come to
the city of Minot (MYE • not). Founded in 1886, Minot
was once a "Wild West" town. There were gunfights in

the streets. Today, Minot is much quieter! Minot State College is in the city. Minot Air Force Base is near Minot.

Head east from Minot. Visit the Geographical (jee • oh • GRAF • ih • kull) Center Museum, at Rugby (RUHG • bee). Do you know what continent the United States is in? It is called North America. The United States, Mexico (MEHKS • ih • koh), and Canada are all part of North America. The very center of North America is near Rugby.

If you go past the far northern edge of North Dakota you will reach another country. It is Canada. The United States and Canada have been friendly neighbors for over

Below: Minot.
Right: This map shows clearly that Rugby, North
        Dakota, is at the very center of North America.

GEOGRAPHIC
CENTER OF
NORTH AMERICA

The International Peace Garden is partly
in North Dakota and partly in Canada.

150 years. The International Peace Garden reminds
people of this. It is partly in Canada and partly in North
Dakota. The flowers remind you of the beauty of peace.

The oldest town in North Dakota is in the
northeastern corner of the state. It is called Pembina. A
fur-trading post was built there in 1797. In 1812 some
families from Canada settled there. They thought they
were in Canada. When the people learned where the
boundary was, they moved back up to Canada.

It's time to finish your North Dakota trip. Go south
along the Red River to the city of Grand Forks. Grand
Forks is in the Red River Valley. It lies where the Red
River meets the Red Lake River.

In the 1870s steamboats traveled on the Red River. Grand Forks grew as a supply station for boats. It was also a stopping-place for oxcarts. Today, Grand Forks is the second biggest city in the Flickertail State.

Grand Forks is one of the state's leading cities for making food products. Sugar beets are grown in the area. They are made into sugar in Grand Forks. Potatoes are grown nearby. They are made into potato chips and french fries in Grand Forks. Wheat fields are nearby. The wheat is made into flour in the city.

Many of the people of North Dakota are of Norwegian (nor • WEE • jun) or Swedish (SWEED • ish) background.

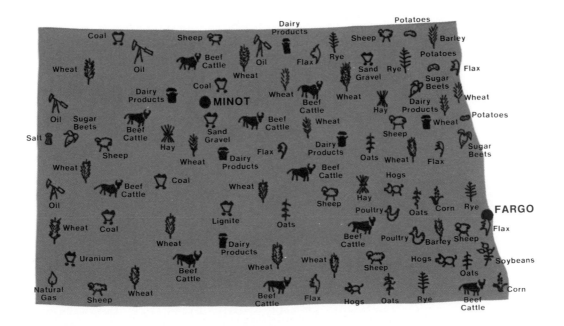

Planes at the Grand
Forks Air Force Base

Would you like to learn about the heritage of these people? You can, at the Scandinavian Cultural (skan • dih • NAY • vee • uhn KULL • chur • ull) Center in Grand Forks.

The University of North Dakota is in Grand Forks. It is the biggest school in the state. Students there study to be doctors and lawyers, teachers and artists.

The Grand Forks Air Force Base is near the city. Missiles (MISS • uhlz) and bombers are kept there.

Places don't tell the whole story of North Dakota. Some interesting people have lived in the Flickertail State.

John Bernard Flannagan (1897?-1942) was born in Fargo. He grew up in an orphanage. He loved to draw. He loved to carve wood. Flannagan became a sculptor.

He carved stone figures of people and animals. His works were put in many United States museums.

Eric Sevareid (SEHV • ah • ride) was born in Velva (VELL • vah), North Dakota in 1912. When he was seventeen, Sevareid made a 2,200-mile canoe trip. A newspaper asked him to write about his adventures. Later, he became a well-known newspaper writer. He also became a famous radio and television reporter.

Lawrence Welk was born in 1903 in Strasburg (STRAHSS • berg), North Dakota. Welk loved music. His father taught him to play the accordion (ah • KORE • dee • uhn). When he was thirteen, Welk played at weddings. Later, Lawrence Welk became famous as the leader of his own band.

Peggy Lee was born near Jamestown, North Dakota, in 1920. She sang in her church choir (KWIRE). She got a job as a singer on a Fargo radio station. She didn't make much money at it. She had to take a job as a bread slicer in a Fargo bakery. But Peggy Lee didn't give up. She became a famous singer.

State Fair, near Minot, after dark

Roger Maris was born in Minnesota in 1934. But he grew up in Fargo, North Dakota. As a boy, he loved to play baseball. He became a big leaguer. Maris was a great home-run hitter. In 1961 Roger Maris hit 61 home runs for the New York Yankees. That's the most homers any baseball player ever hit in one season.

Home to the Sioux Indians . . . then fur traders . . . and now many farm families.

A leading state for growing wheat . . . rye . . . and barley.

A state where you can see the International Peace Garden . . . burning coal beds . . . and the center of North America.

This is the Flickertail State—North Dakota.

Facts About NORTH DAKOTA

Area—70,665 square miles (17th biggest state)

Greatest Distance North to South—210 miles

Greatest Distance East to West—360 miles

Borders—Canada to the north; Minnesota across the Red River to the east; South Dakota to the south; Montana to the west

Highest Point—3,506 feet above sea level (White Butte)

Lowest Point—750 feet above sea level (in Pembina County)

Hottest Recorded Temperature—121°F. (at Steele, on July 6, 1936)

Coldest Recorded Temperature—Minus 60°F. (at Parshall, on February 15, 1936)

Statehood—Our 39th state, on November 2, 1889

Origin of Name North Dakota—The Sioux Indians called themselves the *Dakota,* meaning "friends"; North Dakota was named for that Sioux word

Capital—Bismarck (1889)

Counties—53

U.S. Senators—2

U.S. Representatives—1

State Senators—50

State Representatives—100

State Song—"North Dakota Hymn" by James W. Foley and C.S. Putman

State Motto—*Liberty and Union, Now and Forever, One and Inseparable*

Main Nickname—The Flickertail State

Other Nicknames—The Sioux State, the Peace Garden State, Roughrider Country

State Seal—Adopted in 1889, the year of statehood

State Flag—Adopted in 1911

State Flower—Wild prairie rose

State Bird—Western meadowlark

State Fish—Northern pike

State Fossil—Teredo petrified wood

State Tree—American elm

Some Rivers—Missouri, Little Missouri, Knife, Cannonball, James, Heart, Yellowstone, Red River of the North, Sheyenne, Goose, Forest, Pembina, Souris, Turtle

Largest Lake—Lake Sakakawea (man-made)

National Parklands—Theodore Roosevelt National Memorial Park, Knife River Indian Villages National Historic Site, and Fort Union Trading Post National Historic Site

State Parks and Facilities—14

Animals—White-tailed deer, mule deer, elk, pronghorn antelope, prairie dogs, coyotes, foxes, bobcats, beavers, badgers, skunks, minks, muskrats, raccoons, weasels, flickertail squirrels, buffalo, ducks, geese, grouse, pheasants, partridges, owls, many other kinds of birds

Fishing—Northern pike, bass, trout, perch, catfish, sturgeon, muskie, carp

Farm Products—Wheat, rye, barley, flax, oats, sunflowers, sugar beets, potatoes, soybeans, hay, corn, beef cattle, sheep, hogs, milk, honey, mustard seed, buckwheat, birdseed

Mining—Oil, coal, natural gas, sand, gravel

Manufacturing Products—Many packaged foods, machinery, stone products, clay products, glass products

Population—653,000 (1977 estimate)

Biggest Cities—Fargo   59,000 (1979 estimates)
            Grand Forks   44,200
            Bismarck   42,700
            Minot   33,500
            Jamestown   15,200
            Mandan   14,700

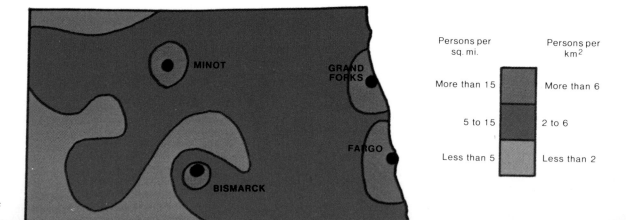

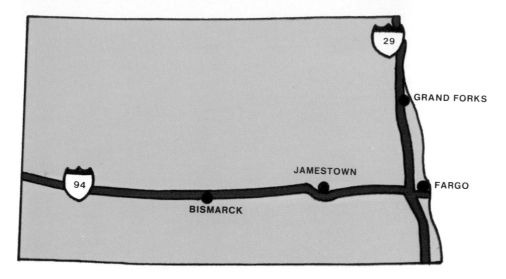

North Dakota History

There were people in North Dakota at least 12,000 years ago.

1682—Frenchman La Salle claims part of what is now North Dakota for
France

1738—Pierre de la Vérendrye, a French-Canadian, is first explorer known to
enter North Dakota

1742—Two of Vérendrye's sons return to the area

1797—The first fur-trading post in North Dakota is built by Charles Chaboillez
at Pembina

1803—By the Louisiana Purchase, the United States takes control of part of
North Dakota from France

1804-1805—Lewis and Clark build Fort Mandan in North Dakota, then spend
the winter there; Indian woman Sacajawea joins them and
guides their trip to the Pacific Ocean

1806—Lewis and Clark pass through North Dakota again on their trip back
east

1812—First settlement in North Dakota is made at Pembina by Irish and
Scottish people from Canada

1818—United States now controls all of North Dakota by getting land from
England

1857—Army establishes Fort Abercrombie, which is its first fort in North
Dakota

1861—Dakota Territory is formed

1871—Fargo is founded

1872—Bismarck is founded

1875—Period of "bonanza" wheat farms begins about now

1876—General George A. Custer leaves Fort Abraham Lincoln for fight
against the Sioux Indians at the Battle of the Little Bighorn, in Montana;
Custer and over 250 of his men are killed

1883—Bismarck becomes capital of the Dakota Territory; Theodore
        Roosevelt starts ranching near Medora
1889—On November 2, North Dakota becomes the 39th state; Bismarck is the
        capital
1890—Fighting between Indians and settlers is over
1897—Flood causes great damage in the Red River Valley
1900—Population of the Flickertail State is 319,040
1914-1918—During World War I, over 31,000 North Dakotans fight for the
        United States; the state supplies food for the United States Army
1915—Nonpartisan League is formed to help farmers
1919—The state-owned Bank of North Dakota is formed at Bismarck
1922—State-owned flour mill opens at Grand Forks
1929—Long period of drought (dry weather) begins and lasts through 1936
1930—Capitol building is destroyed by fire
1932—The International Peace Garden (in both North Dakota and Canada) is
        established
1934—Present state capitol building—the "Skyscraper of the Prairies"—is
        completed
1936—North Dakota's hottest recorded temperature (121°F.) as well as the
        coldest (minus 60°F.) occur in this year
1939-1945—During World War II, over 60,000 North Dakota men and women
        are in uniform; the state supplies much food for the Army
1946—Building begins on the Garrison Dam
1949—Theodore Roosevelt National Memorial Park is dedicated
1951—Oil is found near Tioga
1954—Garrison Dam is completed
1967—Work begins on the Garrison Diversion Project to bring water to a large
        area of North Dakota
1975—About 3½ million people visit North Dakota as tourism becomes more
        and more important.

INDEX

About the Author:

Dennis Fradin attended Northwestern University on a creative writing scholarship and graduated in 1967. While still at Northwestern, he published his first stories in *Ingenue* magazine and also won a prize in *Seventeen's* short story competition. A prolific writer, Dennis Fradin has been regularly publishing stories in such diverse places as *The Saturday Evening Post, Scholastic, National Humane Review, Midwest,* and *The Teaching Paper.* He has also scripted several educational films. Since 1970 he has taught second grade reading in a Chicago school—a rewarding job, which, the author says, "provides a captive audience on whom I test my children's stories." Married and the father of three children, Dennis Fradin spends his free time with his family or playing a myriad of sports and games with his childhood chums.

About the Artists:

Len Meents studied painting and drawing at Southern Illinois University and after graduation in 1969 he moved to Chicago. Mr. Meents works full time as a painter and illustrator. He and his wife and child currently make their home in LaGrange, Illinois.

Richard Wahl, graduate of the Art Center College of Design in Los Angeles, has illustrated a number of magazine articles and booklets. He is a skilled artist and photographer who advocates realistic interpretations of his subjects. He lives with his wife and two sons in Libertyville, Illinois.